Teenage Baseball Umpire: How to Make Great Part-Time Money and Have Fun at Your Job Too

RICH DOSSAN

c/o Produce My Book
PO Box 441024
Aurora, CO 80044
www.ProduceMyBook.com
crew@producemybook.com

CONTENTS

LIFETIME FREE NEXT-STEPS BONUS!

Our aim at Produce My Book is to provide every step, tool, and resource possible for you to take the next step toward becoming a successful youth baseball umpire.

The author, Rich Dossan, has supplied us with a full suite of getting-started documents, recommended videos, game situation quizzes and equipment reviews for your use. We have carefully compiled these valuable resources into a **bonus area** for you to access online whenever you wish.

Some of the bonus items are described in the book, but others are not. So, be sure to get your LIFETIME free access to the bonus area by going to
<u>http://producemybook.com/umpbonusreg</u>

INTRODUCTION

If you are in your mid- to late-teens, like I am, you have a few things on your mind: Making money, enjoying time off, assuring transportation and dating. Sure, school fits in there somewhere; and education is essential. But, school requires us to be there whether you and I want to be or not. All the other luxuries mentioned above require effort to make happen.

Countless other teenagers and I have had to come to terms with getting a part-time job to work after school, on weekends, and over the summers. For many of my friends, the fast food restaurants we chilled at or malls we paced became their choices for employment.

Some of the perks are great (think: free movie tickets and food), but the work is hardly enjoyable when you come home with grease burns from the fries fryer or smell like garbage from cleaning up between the aisles. And, when you finally do get paid, your minimum wage paycheck minus taxes amounts to a little more than a few tanks of gas.

So far, I've been able to avoid the typical jobs for teenagers by working in an industry that has high demand and extraordinarily high hourly rates compared to what my friends have experienced. In my job I work hard, sometimes as much as 12 hours a day, but I get to work outside, be around a sport I love, and, on many occasions, have brought home nearly $400 for two days of work. Now that's great money!

What is this dream job?

Since I was 15 years old, I have been an umpire for local youth baseball leagues and USSSA and Triple Crown tournaments. Before that, I spent most of my weekends playing baseball, beginning with Little League at age 8, then in youth and tournament ball and finally for two years at the high school level.

By sophomore year, I realized two things: I probably wouldn't be a first-string player on the varsity team, if I were to make the team beyond tryouts at all. And, I could make a lot more money as an umpire if my weekends were open. I decided to make umpiring a priority.

Even when I stopped playing baseball and embraced umpiring, I never lost my love for the game, and I think umpiring is the perfect part-time job for teenagers. Maybe it is for you too.

What is a Youth Baseball Umpire?

An umpire officiates the baseball game and is responsible for seeing that the game begins and ends on time, that the teams play a fair game by the rules of the league, and makes judgment calls on plays throughout the match.

That is the dictionary definition.

The reality is that without umpires, baseball games would be mass chaos with fights breaking out and people arguing over whether every pitch was a ball or a strike. What is believed by many to be the greatest sport in the world would be nothing more than a little scrimmage put together in the street – no leagues, no tournaments, no real games at all. It is the umpire that makes baseball an actual game with predictable rules and protocol – a game that kids and adults all love, whether they are playing, coaching, or watching the game.

Wow – That Seems Like Heavy Responsibility – What Kind of Teenager Can Do All That?

Umpiring for youth baseball does carry responsibility, but surprisingly, many teenagers are perfect for the job. This guide will help you understand and develop the skills you need, but before considering umpiring as your summer job, ask yourself the following question: Do you love the game of baseball? I've played ball since I was eight years old in every position on the field. But, you don't have to be a good baseball player to be a good umpire. More important is your affection for the game and interest in and ability to remember the rules and etiquette.

While I played, I learned every rule there is to know about baseball (at least, that's what I thought). I still love to study game situations, techniques, mechanics, and even the rules and regulations. My dad is always trying to catch me with a little known or unusual game situation, but I am just baseball nerdy enough to get them right almost every time.

When I was playing youth league games or attending MLB games, every time I'd see the umpire make a bad call or stand in a wrong position, I would know what was wrong and figured I could do it so much better. And when it comes to fantasy baseball season, let's just say I dominate!

If you have this same passion for the game of baseball, umpiring might be your perfect part-time job.

Advantages of Umpiring include:

1.   Money! - You can expect a broad range of pay depending on the level of baseball you are umpiring and the age of the players, usually between $20 and $50 per game. The older the players, the more money you will make per game. Recreational and city leagues will pay the least, but since those games are shorter than tournament ball, you can still earn a decent hourly rate. Translating games to an hourly rate, you can expect $20-35 per hour, which is a heck of a lot better than what you would earn flipping burgers!

I do most of my umpiring at weekend tournaments now, and have no problem getting 8 or more games to work over a weekend. My parents can hardly believe I can work that many games and still stand on two feet. But, that is one of the benefits of being a teenager. What would be impossible for them is easy for you and me.

Plus, I figure if I'm there already, I may as well be working. You do not get paid for downtime if there is a break between games. On a good weekend, I can make somewhere between $300 and $350, which is 7-8 games. That is more than what a lot of my friends make working every day, all week long, at their part-time minimum wage job. I work for it; that's the truth. But to me, the money is worth it. (And, my dad made me add here that it has helped in saving for my car and college.)

2.   Fun – As a baseball umpire, you get to be around an activity you love. Unless fast food hamburgers or groceries are your passion, most part-time jobs for teens have you spending a significant part of your nights and weekends around something you do not care much about. Umpiring, on the other hand, gives you the opportunity to be involved in something you like and enjoy while earning two or three times the amount per hour than minimum wage provides.

Umpiring is much better than a job inside the kitchen of a fast food restaurant or something like that because you are involved in the game that you have been around, at least, part of your life. It seems like less work than washing dishes because you are outside and not cooped up. Sometimes, baseball umpiring does not even feel like work because the games can get fun when the score is close, and everyone is really into the game.

3. Flexibility – Every week or two, you will get an email from a person called the Assignor. This is the person responsible for staffing umpires for baseball games within a specific league or tournament. You decide how many games you want to work, which days of the week, and if you are available morning, afternoons or evenings. If you want to take a week or two off, the decision is yours! How many of your high school friends can make that claim about their jobs?

4. Availability – There is a national shortage of youth baseball (and softball) umpires. A month after baseball season starts, the lack is even worse. Whereas most summer jobs for teenagers seem very rare, you can sign-up with practically any baseball league or umpire management organization on a Wednesday and get contacted to umpire a game by Saturday. Becoming a baseball umpire could be the most straightforward job to get, and most overlooked, for teenagers!

5. Work Experience - The skills learned and proved by being an umpire look great on college applications and job resumes. In a concise time, you will be able to claim real-world work experience for subjects such as:

- Decision making.
- Leadership.
- Public speaking.
- Attention to detail.
- Conflict resolution.
- Stamina in pressure situations.

6. Compatibility - Umpiring will improve your social skills very quickly because you must talk to all the coaches and even the players and the parents. You will probably be teamed-up with another umpire for the day, and he or she will likely be older than you are. I have worked with partners that were my age all the way up to 70 years old.

No matter how much (or little) you have in common with them, you want to make friends with them because it is no fun to work all day with someone you do not get along with. So, you learn to converse and get along with diverse age groups and types of people, which will help in college, building relationships and at other jobs in your career.

7. Confidence - You do not have to have confidence in yourself to get started as an umpire. But, becoming an umpire will be an excellent way for you to gain confidence in yourself over time.

Showing confidence when calling balls and strikes from behind the plate is essential to reduce challenges made by coaches. But, what sets the tone for a smoothly run game is the way you talk to coaches at the very beginning of the game and tell them what you expect out of them during the game. You must be kind to them, but at the same time be firm to let them know that you know what you are doing on the field. You will be more useful as an umpire if you can make calls firmly and quickly and stand by your decisions.

These are all skills that future employers and colleges want to see in a person.

Disadvantages of Umpiring:

1. Weather - Unless the weather becomes dangerous, the games will go on. I have umpired in 106 degrees under the blistering sun with no wind. The pads you wear working home plate can start to smell like wet gym socks when it's hot, and you can find yourself dripping with sweat for an entire game.

I've umpired in the cold, in the rain, and even in the snow during spring and fall seasons. While most of the time I love to work outside, there are days where it would be much more comfortable to be inside away from the weather.

2. Social Time – You might see your friends less, especially at first. A lot of umpire work is over the weekend, so you might have reduced opportunity to see friends on weekends, which is when they may have free time (if they're not working). Keeping up with other interests as much as you used to might be a challenge like skiing or team sports because you would typically do those activities on weekends. And, that is when the tournaments are.

The flip side to that is that most traditional part-time jobs would have you tied to an even more stringent schedule than umpiring. As an umpire, you can pick the times you want to work, and decline game opportunities in advance that are offered to you, if you are going to do something else that day.

My point is that you will find other times to meet with friends during the week and look for new days and times to enjoy activities from the past. Look for ways to work around the disadvantages.

3. Costs - There are some costs associated with umpiring. While you may be able to borrow some of your gear from the league or other umpires at first, eventually you will need to buy your clothing and umpire gear. The exact equipment you need will be covered later in this guide, but be prepared to invest some money.

4. Volunteer Expectations

- You may feel pressure to volunteer occasionally. Umpires get paid for regular season games. However, if the league you are working for is affiliated with the official "Little League," you will likely be asked to volunteer for one or two post-season tournament games. No umpires working the Little League World Series tournament can accept payment for their hours spent. This tradition has evolved in part because the National Little League organization is a non-profit organization. The volunteerism aspect is also supposed to reduce favoritism and bias during the umpiring process.

Instead of thinking of volunteering as a negative and just working for free, consider it an honor to be invited to serve. Volunteering displays a sense of gratitude in what you have been given in your paid work. Plus, umping World Series games, even at the lowest levels, is still tournament play. So, you will enjoy the higher quality of players.

Umpiring as a volunteer can also open the gates to working tournaments in other leagues where you will get paid. People who schedule umpires in one league usually know the schedulers for tournaments in different leagues. You can easily enter those tournaments as an umpire by getting referred from a scheduler in another league.

Also, if your high school is anything like mine, you will be required to show that you put in community service hours to graduate. Volunteering to umpire a few games is an excellent way to earn those hours. Just do not make the same mistake I made the first time I volunteered. Make sure to have your assignor sign your community service certificate, so you get credit for it!

5. Challenge - Even though the title of this book includes "good money," you will likely discover umpiring to be a lot more difficult than you thought it would be. Umpiring a baseball game is a lot more of a science than ballplayers might believe. There are a lot of specific mechanics that an umpire does to be where they need to be to get the full vision of play and make the right calls.

Some people will never learn what they need to advance beyond umpiring recreational and city leagues and work for the competitive and tournament game leagues. While some people would see this as a negative to the job, I hope that you will consider it an advantage.

The benefits of umpiring are many, and the drawbacks are few. The one aspect of umpiring that is like any other job is that you will grow with it the more you do it. Umpiring baseball games will quickly become a part of you. You will get to know other umpires, and you will be soon accepted as part of an exclusive team that manages the baseball game on the field.

Try not to be too nervous about getting started, but instead look forward to it. I'm going to help you with every step in the pages that follow. You are about to learn the valuable skills you will need to get more involved with the best game in the world; the game of baseball! And, those skills you will use as an umpire, or in any other career, for the rest of your life.

PART 1: BASICS THAT WILL HELP YOU AS AN UMPIRE

Don't even think about being an umpire if you do not enjoy being around baseball. Umpiring is not the job for everyone. But, if you do like baseball, it could be the one for you. You do need a few other skills too, however, to make it fun as well as worthwhile.

Physical Stamina

Umpiring is usually easier for younger people than older because you do have to have some level of physical endurance. I've seen a lot of very out of shape umpires. Health and age do not necessarily affect a person's ability to be a good umpire, but being in shape or not affects an umpire's performance.

Be prepared that you will be standing all day. I mean, you cannot just go sit down on the job in the middle of an inning! You do not even get to sit on the bench as players can in the dugout between innings. You will be standing the whole game, and in the summer the temperature will be at its hottest in your part of the country. You must be able to deal with the sun.

Umpiring does involve running even if you have not ever noticed an umpire running during a game before. You must do squats on the home plate. While being physically fit might not influence how other umpires, coaches or players will think of you, being in decent shape will be to your benefit and will make the job easier.

Toughness

Together with physical stamina is general toughness. There will be situations where the ball hits you, especially when you are behind the plate. You do not get to hold a glove. And getting hit by a ball pitched by an eight-year-old kid hurts almost as much as getting hit by a ball thrown by an eighteen-year-old. It hurts! A good umpire needs to stand there and take it because the call is more important than your bodily health.

Some people get hit by pitches more than others. I have not gotten smacked by a ball often, but I know one umpire that gets hit like three times every day. It's weird. It's like some people are ball magnets and others are not. But you cannot be an umpire and not get hit by a ball eventually.

When a ball hits you, you will need to be tough and still stay in the game. The teams, coaches, and especially your umpire partner, are counting on you to finish the game. Umpiring competitive or tournament games is not easy to umpire alone. You could switch positions with your partner and work the field, but the coaches and players get used to your strike zone and call strategy, and they will not like it if you switch in the middle of the game. They might seem understanding, but they are not going to be thrilled about the switch and could even dispute the game results later. Better to tough it out if your injury is not severe.

Getting Along With People

Your whole job as an umpire is around people, so being able to get along with them is important. And you must be able to deal with people disagreeing with you and even yelling at you and still stand your ground. Being able to get along with different people is essential—especially those who are older than you are.

If you are already the kind of person that can meet people for the first time and get along well with them, that skill will make umpiring much more comfortable for you. It makes your experience better for your umpiring partners as well. There are various people you will get paired up with, of all ages, and you usually spend the entire day with them. Make an effort to be able to get along with them no matter what kind of person they are.

Focus

Umpiring is not the job for daydreamers. A two-hour game is a long time to be focused every second, primarily if you are working in the field position (as opposed to the home plate position). Honestly, in some games (especially recreational league games) staying focused in the field is not easy, especially when the pitcher throws ball after ball. If the game rules prohibit stealing bases, you are just standing there waiting for the crack of a bat. Then you finally have something to do.

When I am working that kind of game in the field, I do the same trick that coaches teach their fielders sometimes. Every pitch I walk around a little circle. I watch the ball then I do a short two to three step walk-around. It keeps me moving in the field and keeps my focus a bit more than just standing still.

The good news is that as you move up and work more competitive leagues and tournament ball, the games become more engaging and are active enough that, if you are not a daydreamer by nature, you will have no problem focusing and following the game.

Confidence

Using a loud and firm voice to show your confidence will make your experience as an umpire much easier. People will pick up on hesitancy. Even if you are not sure of a call, act like you are. There are going to be close plays where the call could go either way. Have the confidence to make the call and stick with it. The league hired you, not the coaches or the parents, to call the game. So, that is what you need to do.

My first umpiring mentor told me, "A play is nothing until the umpire calls it." Have the confidence to do your best and stick with it. Blowing a call is not the worst thing to ever happen. How you handle yourself throughout the game is what matters.

PART 2: GETTING THE JOB

I mentioned earlier that if you want to become an umpire, it a pretty easy gig to get no matter where you are in the country. Look at any ball field and, if games are being played, they are going to need umpires. They always seem to need more umpires.

Getting a summer or part-time job as an umpire is not hard, but the way to do it is a little different than walking into your nearest fast food restaurant and asking for an application.

I highly suggest you start umpiring at a recreational league level. In tournament ball, the coaches and parents and even the players can get pretty riled up, so if you do not know what you are doing yet, and how to react when basic situations occur, you will likely get discouraged quickly.

Learning the ropes at the recreational level is the best training ground. Although the pay is lower than for tournament ball or competitive leagues, rec leagues often hire younger kids, so you may be able to get your first job before you turn sixteen. In general, the coaches do not expect tournament level umpires in recreational leagues, so they will be more forgiving when you miss calls.

Recreational leagues usually have one staff member who supervises the entire sports program. You must find that person. If he has an assignor or scheduler who hires the umpires, he will put you in touch with the right person.

How do you find that guy?

It was easy for me because I played in the recreational city league where I lived, and my dad coached. The supervisor had not changed, so my dad did me a favor and sent him an email to see who I should talk to and a phone number. Before I could even make a phone call, the director called me! I was in business. So, step one for you to use your connections.

That same summer I worked for a competitive Little League too. I got that job by talking to an old friend whose dad was coaching a team in that league. My friend gave me the number of the assignor, and when I called, he asked me to come by on opening day. I ended up working two games before I even completed the paperwork!

My point is that while you won't often find umpiring jobs in traditional advertisements or on "help wanted" signs, youth baseball leagues need a constant supply of good umpires. Once you get that first game, the rest will follow like nothing if you do an excellent job.

What if I have no connections?

If you do not have a parent or a friend with the connections you need, it takes a little extra effort to find the right person to hire you. But it is not hard. First, try the website for whatever league is closest to where you live. If it is a city recreational league, you may need to start with the city's website and find the area of the site related to youth sports. The website will probably have contact information for baseball leagues. Call that number and explain you are interested in umpiring in the league and ask for the name of the supervisor. In most cases, doing this will get you in contact with the right person.

If all else fails, visit the ball fields where you want to work and ask one of the umpires you see working there. Most likely they will either point out the supervisor, and you can talk to him or her on the spot. Or, the umpire will probably have the person's phone number by cell phone.

Is it that easy? It sounds like they would give the job to anyone!

Well, that is not the case. When you do talk to the supervisor or assignor about becoming an umpire, they will ask you some qualifying questions, mostly about how much baseball you have played, for how long and at what levels. If one of your parents coached in the league or you are still friendly with a coach you played for, be ready to mention a name or two.

Remember, you do not have to be a star baseball player to be a good umpire. That is not what is being asked of you.

What needs to be known is that you have a grasp of the rules and etiquette for the game of baseball and that you have confidence in your voice with the potential to handle yourself in a game. Mostly, the supervisor is looking for why you are interested in umpiring in the first place.

PART 3: I GOT THE JOB! NOW WHAT?

Training

You will likely be provided with some initial training, but be prepared to learn as you go. City recreational leagues might have one or two training sessions you must attend, but most learning is on the job. You can always sign up for seminars and clinics on your own, but they cost money you have not earned yet. So formal, professional-grade training is probably not something you should expect or seek right away.

When I first started umpiring, I worked my first couple of games with my assignor. I just showed up on opening day in the clothes he told me to wear, which was gray umpire pants, black socks, black sneakers, black belt and a tee shirt to wear under the shirt.

My assignor started by telling me where to go in certain

game situations and explained a few unusual league rules. We talked a lot between innings and games, and he went over things that happened in the game, and I could ask questions and stuff. He supplied me with the equipment I needed for the first few games, but eventually, I was required to buy my own. After we both decided it was a job I could do, and I wanted to continue, he assigned me to work with a more senior umpire for a while who would enjoy showing me the ropes.

Be Willing to Learn More

I mentioned earlier that I thought I knew baseball well, sometimes better than the umpires in a game. Well, I learned very quickly that there are a lot of particular rules that no one knows except for umpires. As one example, when you are working the plate and a batter squares up to bunt, you must know when to call a pitch a strike or a ball. Obviously, if the bat moves forward, it is a strike. But, some people think you must pull back for it to be called a ball. But, if the batter stays squared up and the bat doesn't move at all, it does not count as a swing, and the umpire should call based on where the pitch falls in the strike zone.

My assignor taught me a lot of things that most players would not think about that could come up in a game. As I started working with more senior umpires, they did the same. We would play a game called "test the umpire," and they would give me all kinds of weird scenarios to see how I would handle it.

At first, I was amazed when I answered almost every pop quiz incorrectly! And I thought I knew baseball well. Now

I know the answers and am often stumping new umpires with the same questions. So, I guess putting me on the spot like that paved the way for me to learn what I needed to know to help me make the right calls.

My point is this: If you start off thinking you know your stuff, and find out you do not, there is still hope for you! And it does not matter how much you know. There will always be those occurrences that happen once every four years or something. But, when it does happen, it blows up in your face if you do not know the proper call. So, learn everything you can, even if you have never seen specific situations happen in games before.

Gear You Will Need

In recreational leagues, you can probably borrow the equipment you will need for a few games as I mentioned before. If you decide to continue umpiring, you will want to invest some of your first earnings into gear. You will need it to work more competitive leagues and tournament ball (which pay more), so you may as well get the gear early, so you are ready. You cannot continue long-term to ask other umps to borrow their equipment. At higher levels, you are expected to have your own gear.

I borrowed some money from my parents to get the basics and paid it back within a couple of months as a percentage of what I earned. Maybe your family will be willing to do the same for you too. You can also save money by shopping at used or discount sporting goods stores or even a thrift store for the pants and shoes. You will need to buy a lot of the gear on the internet that is unique to an umpire. However, if you live in an area where baseball is very popular, then you may be able to find a more traditional umpire supply store nearby.

Make sure to register for your **LIFETIME FREE NEXT STEPS BONUS** to find links to recommended gear and websites that will help you get started. Visit **http://producemybook.com/umpbonusreg**

Here is a list of the equipment you will need to get as soon as possible, and some extra stuff that you will want to consider getting over time:

1. Umpire Shirts - I was told by my supervisor to get a dark blue shirt and a light blue shirt. Umpire shirts are collared and are made large and stretchy enough to fit over chest pads. New, the shirts will cost around $45 each. I got my first two shirts at a second-hand sports store called Play-It-Again Sports for about $15 each. Later, when I started working a lot of tournaments, I added a black shirt because a lot of the other umpires wanted to wear black (if you pair with another umpire you will want to wear the same colors).

2. Umpire Pants - Formal umpire pants have stretchy material that allows them to flex with movement and provide room for pads underneath. Prices range from $40-$75 depending on the features you want. I bought two pairs of gray dress pants at a thrift store in a size larger than I usually wear for $5 each. I am still using one pair of those pants four years later. I had a pen leak in the pocket of the other pair, and I had to throw it away. That was a lot easier to take knowing it only cost me five bucks. As far as I can tell, no one has ever noticed that I'm not wearing "official" umpire pants.

3. Umpire Hat - Yes, umpire hats are different than regular baseball caps and regular cap stores do not sell them. Plate hats have a shorter brim so that you can fit the mask over it. There are different hats for the field with a wider rim. You do sweat a lot at the plate, so I recommend that you get both, especially if you are working the plate and the field during the same day. That way you will feel cleaner and less sweaty when you are in the field. Get black to begin, and you may want to add a navy hat eventually. Hats cost $15-30.

4.   Shoes - Eventually, you want to have both field shoes and plate shoes, which have a reinforced toe in case your foot gets hit by the ball (which happens a lot). When I first started, I just bought a pair of black sneakers at the thrift store for $10. As soon as I could, however, I purchased field shoes. While field shoes are like sneakers, they are built better for the movements an umpire makes in the field, and have some reinforcement to protect your feet from stray balls. Your feet hurt a lot less after a day of umpiring in field shoes rather than cheap sneakers.

I did not buy plate shoes until my third year of umpiring, but am glad I finally did! I would not recommend wearing plate shoes on the field, though, as they are too stiff for sprinting from play to play comfortably. Plus, plate shoes just look weird on an umpire working the field. Both field and plate shoes cost anywhere from $65 to over $200 depending on the brand and features you choose.

5. Black Socks - Use high black baseball socks. Even though they will not be visible to anyone, the shin pads you wear behind the plate can chafe under your knees if you are not wearing high socks. You can get a 2-pack of baseball socks for about $8.

6. Black Belt - You will need a black dress belt, and I recommend you buy one just for umpiring because you are sweating so much while you work. Do not use the stretchy black baseball belts you would wear as a player! An umpire should wear the more formal looking dress belt.

7. Face Mask, Chest, Shoulder and Shin Pads - You can borrow these for a while, but you will want to get your own as soon as possible. By buying your own, you can adjust them to fit your body correctly, which is safer, more comfortable, and faster to assemble.

Some umpires will use catcher's gear, but if you are going to umpire for a while and get into higher game levels, you should invest in chest guards specifically for umpiring. They are harder and will protect you better than catcher's gear. Remember, they do not let you hold a glove back there to defend yourself from stray pitches! The equipment is a worthwhile investment. Expect to spend $100 minimum for a full assembly. You will be tempted to buy umpire gear kits with all the pieces, but kits are lower quality overall. You will be better off buying each piece of gear separately for best quality and fit.

8. Accessories - You will also need a strike and ball clicker, plate brush and a ball bag. You can get a kit that includes all these things for about $10-$15. You might want to buy a kit to start and replace with higher quality accessories as you need to or can financially afford.

9. Jacket - An umpire jacket is not mandatory, but nice to have in the fall and spring seasons when it can be cold and rainy. There are a lot of cool jacket options, and you will probably want to add one at some point. They are $50 or more depending on what you want. I did not buy a jacket until my third year of umpiring. It sure paid for itself as it was a pretty wet spring that year and I was working extra games to save up for college.

Gear can set you back anywhere from $150 - $400 depending on what deals you can find. It sounds like a chunk of change to put out, but all I can tell you is it was worth it to me to do it. I have made it back repeatedly, and I have only had to replace a few things like socks, the pants I ruined and a clicker. The rest still works fine five years later. And there is no reason preventing you from just getting the basics to start and build on as you earn money.

Most teenagers who work in a fast food restaurant or retails store in the mall spend part of their earnings on shoes or clothes too. So, umpiring should not be thought of as different in this regard, other than the fact you will not see me wearing my plate shoes or umpire shirt to school or the movies! I invested in my future and am now making more money than they are and loving what I do.

Paperwork

You will be asked to fill out a little paperwork before you are paid and will probably need to provide some form of identification, such as a driver's license, birth certificate or social security card.

When you interview, make sure to find out whether you will be an employee or a contractor because there are differences. As an employee, the league will deduct any taxes you owe. If you are a self-contractor, you are responsible for your taxes (and can claim expenses, such as your gear). Depending on how much you earn in a year, you may or may not owe taxes. This is an area where you might want to ask your parents for a little help.

Every baseball league I've worked has hired me as a contractor except for one city recreational league, which brought me on initially as a city employee. That was fun because I also got free use of the city pool and rec center like any other part-time city worker would. I had to take a short city employee training class and even pass a simple written examination. They also required me to get a physical from my doctor. After all of that, they too moved to the self-contractor structure a year later.

The good news is if you are working with a league that uses ArbiterSports.com, you only have to do the paperwork once, and it works for all leagues that use the online scheduler.

PART 4: GETTING READY FOR THE GAME

Most leagues hire an assignor to manage the umpires for the league's games. A lot of assignors work for several different leagues or tournaments, and they try to recruit a large group of umpires they can call on to fill all the games coming up.

The assignor is your manager/boss, although you may not see the assignor every time that you work. If the assignor works for more than one league, you may be assigned to different leagues or tournaments every week depending on where the games are and your availability. I highly suggest you make yourself as available as you can at first. Once you develop the reputation with your assignor of being reliable, showing up and doing an excellent job, you will have no shortage of opportunities to work.

Your assignor will contact you by phone, email or text. He will confirm that you are available and then assign you to a game he needs to fill. Usually, for a tournament weekend, you will be asked for your availability for both Saturday and Sunday. You will probably be granted the opportunity to choose one or the other, both days, or just the morning of one day and all day the next, or whatever you need to fit your schedule. Usually, I just say full availability, and they'll give me 7 to 10 games over the weekend.

Unless you are working for lower level recreational leagues, you will likely work with a partner, where one works home plate while the other works in the field. The assignor will probably assign who covers the plate or the outfield, but if not, just work that out with your assigned partner before the game. If you have two or more games in a day, switch positions every game, so workloads are evenly distributed.

If the league only budgets for one umpire per game (recreational leagues or tee-ball levels, usually), you will probably earn a little more money to work the game alone. You will need to move around a lot more trying to see everything in the field as well as running the plate. I don't think the little bit of extra money is worth it. No one likes umpiring games alone, and you will never do as good of a job. That is why you will almost never be called upon to umpire a higher-level game without a partner.

Sports Management Website (e.g., Arbiter Sports)

While some city leagues manage their umpire schedules manually and independently from other web-based systems, you will probably be asked to start an account with a particular online scheduler. Expect this for sure when you start working with an assignor who works for more than one organization. An example that is becoming widely used by many leagues throughout the U.S. is a sports management system called ArbiterSports.com.

ArbiterSports.com is used to manage leagues and officials for all different sports and competitive levels, not just umpiring. Most organizations use it.

Assignors use the sports management site to assign and evaluate games. And, most important (at least to me) it is used to pay the umpires. I like to be paid through ArbiterSports.com because no matter what league or tournament organization I am working for, I get paid electronically once a week. All I must do is sign onto the site and transfer my wages to my bank account. With the recreational league, I wait for up to three weeks to receive a mailed check, which is a real pain compared to the online way.

An assignor might contact you by email, phone or text as well as through the online scheduler. But you still need to go in and accept the game to be paid.

While an assignor may assign games on short notice, you usually get asked about your availability a week in advance of the games. The assignor then assigns you to matches based on your reply, and you accept or decline them. Once you take a game, you are assigned your partner and given directions to the field and what time you must show up. This is all done through the online management tools.

Be ready for times where the league or the tournament

organization does not coordinate with the assignor well enough for you to know everything in advance. Your assignor may ask you to work at the last minute, or you will know you are working but no details are supplied until the last minute.

When that happens, you just work the assigned games and accept them after the fact within the online management tool. It's not a big deal, but something you need to remember to do so that you will get paid! The important thing is to stay in touch with the assignor and be accessible and available when they reach out to you. Oh, and to get paid. Did I mention that already?

Game Day

Not to sound like a drag, but I suggest not staying out too late or party hard the night before you are scheduled to umpire. The day is just a whole lot better if you are alert and ready to go. Being sharp and substance-free is your responsibility and your way of offering respect to the game and being an excellent example for the players.

I would suggest you show up about a half an hour before your scheduled game. Be sure to go to the bathroom when you arrive because umpires do not get bathroom breaks during games.

Next, you will want to head to your field and find your partner. Make sure you have checked your schedule to learn your assigned ball field, your partner's name and his or her cell number. If your partner is not there and hasn't phoned or texted yet, make the first move and reach out. Just say, "Hey, this is Rich, your partner for the day. Just want to know what color you're wearing." That's an easy, unforceful way of asking for a response so that you will have some comfort knowing that your partner is on the road. Although, most usually do show up (sometimes at the last minute) regardless of if we'd been in contact before.

When I first started umpiring, I would get excited before a game, just like when I was playing on a team. But over time, I stopped anticipating games in the same way because I had learned to treat it as a job. But then, as the game goes on it starts to get exciting again, and fun. That is quite cool because I know my friends that are working at fast food do not feel that way about scraping grills or scrubbing toilet bowls at their jobs!

There are always those blowout games and some with less skilled players that are boring to umpire. As an official, you are not invested in the teams, so it can get pretty dull. The good news is if you put in your time on the boring games and learn as much as you can, you will eventually be assigned the more advanced and fun games to work.

You will never forget the day you are assigned to work your first tournament championship game. There are usually more than 100 spectators and the championship game of the weekend is generally under lights. Although you are paid the same, as if it is any other ordinary game, you know it's something special for the kids. You will not be assigned to a tournament championship by accident or before you're ready. I can assure you that the excitement of umpiring a championship youth baseball game for the first time will make all those lower level games, where you struggled to focus, worth the effort and patience.

Plate and Field Umpiring

If you are the field umpire, your job is mainly to call plays that occur at the bases. The plate umpire stands behind home plate and calls the strikes and balls, strikeouts and walks, as well as any plays at the home base. If the league wants the umpires to keep track of the score on official scorecards, the plate umpire will be the one to do that. Just as an aside, always have a pen handy for this purpose. The league always seems to have the scorecard ready, but never a spare pen.

Sometimes, your assignor will tell you if you are scheduled to work in the field or behind home plate. If he does not, you and your partner just need to work it out. If I have the choice, I like to work behind home plate first, while I am fresh.

Working behind home plate is more mentally challenging than to work the field. Standing in the field is a bit more chilled, so it can feel less like work and more like you are in the game. But, calls at the bases can happen fast and are often harder to judge, so you must stay with the game and be ready to move around and follow it.

For example, when there is no one on base, you position yourself behind first base on the baseline, about 15 feet beyond the base toward right field. If a batter hits a double, however, you must run to the center of the field or run to where you can best see the play and make the call at second. If you stay standing at the first baseline and make the call at second base, you may not have an unobstructed view of the play, and it could be disputed.

There are a lot of different scenarios for what can happen, and it would take a lot of time to go through them all, but proper mechanics for working both in the field and behind the plate should be something you learn as you go from your first trainer and senior umpires.

The **LIFETIME FREE BONUS AREA** has videos, quizzes and other resources to help you learn proper umpiring positioning and mechanics. Visit **http://producemybook.com/umpbonusreg** to get started for free.

There are specific legal appeals that a coach can follow to have one umpire ask the other if his call was right. But if the umpire did everything correctly to get the best view and the play was just hard to call, the umpire will usually agree with the call. Make sure you learn the proper positioning and stick with the game to avoid putting your partner in the position of having to judge your call.

Pregame Meeting

Starting the game on time is the umpire's responsibility. So, walk to the home plate a few minutes before the scheduled start time and call what is announced as a coaches meeting. If there are multiple games on the field, try to start the game a couple of minutes early to keep things on schedule. The coaches can choose to hold off on your attempt to start early if they have a good reason. But, it's weird, starting even three or four minutes early each game will keep the entire day on schedule, while starting a bit late can back everything up. Coaches need to agree to start a little early. We can't force it. But they are usually ready to go and have been warming up for some time, and it's not a problem.

Coaches always seem to take forever to come to the plate for the meeting, which is another reason I like to go out there a little early to get them started. They always have to go back to get baseballs or lineups or something else. If the coaches do not see you standing there, you will have to call out loudly, "Coaches! Home plate please!" and that will move them.

Once we are all gathered, I ask the coaches to verify the lineup card if there is one. Then I will confirm whether batting will be lineup players only or the whole team. Some leagues have every player bat even if some are sitting on the bench. Others will just let those players assigned a field position to hit. Rec league rules usually require all players to be included in a continuous lineup. If the home and away teams have not been assigned, we flip a coin for it at this meeting.

Then I make sure the coaches are aware of specific league rules like what the mercy rule is and how many times a coach can talk to a pitcher. You will be issued a rule book, or at least a few pages of specific rules and guidelines, for the league you are umpiring. So, you should be stating these rules because you know them officially. Then I let them know what to do if they have a problem with a call, confirm that if it is a judgment call, it is non-negotiable, and let them know anything else we expect of them.

The plate meeting happens fast but sets the tone that you know what you are doing and that you expect everyone to respect you and your calls. You will have a better all-around game if you approach the meeting with confidence and authority.

Finally, we shake hands and say good luck. The game clock starts at the completion of the coaches meeting at home plate.

The home team will usually elect to take the field first, but not always. Sometimes even coaches get confused as to which team gets to bat in the last inning. So, make sure you are aware which team is starting in the field and at-bat.

The, stand to the side while the pitcher warms up. League rules will state how many warm-up pitches are allowed at the beginning of the pitcher's first inning versus additional innings. You and your umpire partner should stand at the sideline and are free to drink some water and talk about whatever you'd like. But, be sure to keep a count of the warm-up pitches so that the game stays on track.

When both teams are in position, and you are working behind the plate, you get to start the game with a loud and confident, "Play ball!"

PART 5: GAME TIME

Obstructions

Throughout the game, you need to be watching for possible interference as well as the gameplay. For instance, coaches and players are supposed to stay inside the dugout to prevent being hit by a ball in play. If a poorly thrown ball hits the defensive coach standing inside the fence, it is an automatic safe base for the runner.

You also want to make sure the first baseman is not standing on the base obstructing the runner from getting around him. And keep an eye out for extra balls on the field or someone tying their shoe and stuff like that. As soon as you are aware of a possible interference, just call time out and take care of it.

Interaction with Players

I am always friendly around the ballplayers, but you do not want to talk with kids so much that you give the impression of favoritism toward any one team. Even if you know someone on a team, be careful not to chat a lot with the person. During the game, you are making calls, and the players are playing the game, so avoid trying to have a lot of one-on-one personal interaction. You are there for an important reason, and it's not to socialize.

Catchers may talk to the umpire, and you want to be polite and friendly if they do. Every once in a while if a catcher makes a good warm-up throw to second base feel free to compliment him. But, remember your primary job is to officiate the game. So keep your focus on that.

Interaction with Coaches

Be friendly and chat with the coaches as they pass. I sometimes joke with them between innings. They will always laugh at your jokes because they want to make a good impression on you!

When play is in progress, you will only talk to a coach if there is a dispute with a call. Coaches may challenge any call, even if it is clear to everyone else watching. If a call does not go a team's way, their coach will not be happy about it and may argue it no matter what the correct call was. That is just something you must handle. Stay with the call, unless you know you were wrong, and it makes a material difference (for example, you call a runner safe on a forced out). If it is just a judgment call, stick with your original call. Being uncertain makes you appear less in control of the game.

You just have to know you will never please both teams all the time for an entire game. One of the teams will disagree with you at some point. What matters is that, at the end of the game, you think you did a pretty good job. But both teams will rarely be pleased with you at the same time.

If a coach becomes troublesome during a game, there is a particular disciplinary process for handling them. It's hard sometimes, but you must know that you are the umpire, and need to stay in control of the game. In general, most coaches follow the protocol of the game, and if one gets out of hand, the assistant coaches or parents in the dugout will calm them down before you reach the end of the disciplinary process. They are setting a bad example for the players, and usually, someone has a cool enough head to keep them in line. If not, here are the steps you would take:

1.   Ignore - If a coach is nagging you about something like your strike zone, your first step is to do nothing. Again, you are in control of the game and the plays, and you don't have any obligation to listen to a coach's opinion.

2.   Acknowledge - If the coach continues despite your ignoring them, rip off your mask and acknowledge him with a look and the words "that's enough."

3.   Give an official warning - If the coach persists, provide them with a formal warning. All you do is say, "Coach, that is enough, this is your one and only official warning." Usually, you never have to get beyond this step. The other coaches and parents will probably have them cooled down by now, but if not…

4.   Restrict them to the dugout - Say "that's enough - I'm restricting you to the bench - I don't want to hear another word out of you." They must sit (not stand) on the bench in the dugout, and they can stay in the dugout and cheer on the team, but you don't want to hear any more complaining. If you do…

5.   Throw them out of the game - If the coach can't stay seated and quiet in the dugout (other than cheering for the team), that's the end of that. Tell them to leave the field. They are ejected from the game. If they don't exit the field, stop the game clock and call every kid off the field until he does. If he refuses to leave, then his team forfeits the game.

Umpires go through the process of disciplining coaches without bringing in tournament or league management. You only need to report the incident afterward to your assignor who lets the league know.

Dealing with out-of-line coaches gets easier as you become more experienced as an umpire. You start to learn the boundaries that a coach can stay within, and you get a better feel for when they cross the line. You also get more comfortable with the five-step process, and it is easier to follow it the more accustomed you are to it.

You might think that as you work with the same coaches over time, you will know how they will react in a game, but it is different depending on if they are winning or losing. The same coach may be happy with you, and everything is good, but then the next game when he's losing he might turn on you. Some are all around nice guys all the time, but most will act negatively toward the umpires if things don't go their way. You cannot take the fact that they are winning or losing into consideration, though. If they are saying stuff to you, you must deal with it whether they are losing or winning.

The five-step process does work most of the time. I've only worked about two games in the five years I have been an umpire where we have had to eject a coach. It doesn't happen often at all. But after they leave, we just say "Let's play ball!" in an upbeat voice. It may seem strange at the time, but you will usually get applause from the parents of both sides because they all hated the situation as well!

Weather

Most new umpires are surprised to learn that continuing or delaying play in inclement weather situations is not usually the umpire's call. The league supervisor will come over to tell us that they spotted lightening nearby on their phone's weather app and ask you to call in the kids. Once they tell us that the teams can resume play, the game continues. So, while it may seem like the umpires make the decision, that is usually not the case.

On the other hand, if inclement weather causes hazardous field conditions, stopping or continuing play is the umpire's call. For instance, you can play in the mud, but you must look at how kids are executing routine plays. If the kids are having trouble just picking up easy grounders or easy pop flies because they're slipping in the mud when they try to make plays, we might pull them in for a while and try to dry it out a little bit with quick dry in the dangerous areas. If that doesn't help and it is still hazardous for routine play, it is the umpire's call whether to stop the game.

Game Over!

There isn't a lot more to do after a game is over. The coaches shake hands, and their team lines up for high-fives. Most of the time the coaches and teams include umpires in this routine, and we shake hands and high five everyone. It's funny when a team thinks we did a bad umpiring job and they ignore us by not shaking our hands thinking they are sending us a message about their disapproval and insulting us. The truth is most umpires do not care what the coaches, players or parents think of their officiating performance. If they come over, we are happy to shake and high five, but if not, we are just moving on to the next game.

I once saw a player's mother run onto the field after the game and threatened to "beat the *$&@!" out of the umpire. Had she touched him, he could have had her arrested for assault! Fortunately, another parent chased after the woman and settled her down. The umpire left the field promptly for his car. Know that this kind of parent aggression is infrequent. The longer you hang around the field, the higher the opportunity for comments to start and tensions to continue. After the game, get to the next game you are assigned to or to someplace away from the parents and teammates.

Finally, you may be required to complete the scorecard and sign it. Some leagues require you to get signatures from the head coaches of both teams as well. You give the scorecard to the league supervisor so that they can update the brackets, and your job is over for that game.

Things to Expect Early On in Umpiring

Umpiring is a job that you grow into over time, which is why it is a good idea to start in the recreational or city leagues until you get used to some things that will seem unexpected at first. Here are few things to expect:

• **You will sound strange to yourself** - In your first few games, you are probably going to think to yourself that you sound weird making calls out loud. I remember thinking initially that there was no way I sounded like an umpire. I probably did fine, but it seemed very awkward at first. Expect that and just try to accept that you will feel uncomfortable. Work toward creating your style and voice, which will help you feel more normal calling plays.

• **You will worry about how you look** - The first time you serve as the plate umpire, you will feel like everyone is looking at you. When you go into your first squat, you will barely bend your knees, thinking the parents behind the backstop will start laughing at your position. Get over this insecurity quickly. Realize right now that no one is looking at you. They are all paying attention to the batter and where the ball goes once it's pitched. You must get into the correct positions to see the pitches and plays correctly and ignore any thoughts you have about people watching you. Although you and I know how important the role of an umpire is to a baseball game, spectators see you as something blocking their view, and that's all.

- **Be loud and firm** - Practice speaking louder and stronger than you think is necessary. At first, it will feel like you are too loud, but people expect loudness, confidence, and clarity from the umpire. Make your gestures and body language firm, robust and consistent as well, so that everyone can follow the game. I had one mentor tell me that you need to call a game as though someone who is blind or deaf will know precisely what's going on in the game by what they see or hear. That was great advice that I still remember and practice to this day.

- **Mechanics** - Take the time to learn the essentials of umpire mechanics as quickly as you can. You will be learning new mechanics all the time, but the sooner you learn the basics of calling at home plate or where to run in the field to follow the plays, the more comfortable you will feel in the role of umpire. Movements, gestures, and positioning can best be showed visually, which is why I've assembled a collection of videos and images for you to study in the **LIFETIME FREE BONUS AREA.** Visit **http://producemybook.com/umpbonusreg** to get started.

- **Learn the rules** - If you are umpiring in a new league or tournament, make sure to find out the specific rules of the league before you start calling the game. You do not want to be asking coaches or parents what the mercy rule is or when coach pitch applies, for example. That just makes you look like an amateur and less in control of the game.

PART 6: HANDLING CHALLENGES AND IMPROVING OVER TIME

Patience

Patience is a challenge you will have to deal with regularly to get better as a teenage umpire. Here are a few areas where you will need to be patient that I discovered along the way:

Coaches - The thing to remember with coaches is that, while you need to hold your temper with them and always stay in control, you do not need to be patient with them. You oversee the game, and you can do whatever you want with the coaches.

With that said, understand that a game is no fun for anyone when there are a lot of controversies. So, it is best if you hold your temper and just follow the five steps to dealing with a problem coach without adding any emotion to the situation. That takes some patience but comes with time as you get more confident in your role as an umpire.

Yourself - At first, you must be patient with yourself. For a while, it will feel like you make more mistakes than you should, and it would be easy to get impatient and just quit. But your skills will improve as time goes on and you will start seeing many situations occurring over and over, which will become easier to recognize and deal with. You will get better if you stick to it and umpiring will become easier the more you do it.

Age Group and Skill Set of the Teams - At first, I was willing to umpire any age group and any skill set because I was just learning. But once you start to get better and more used to being an umpire, it can become tiring to work games with young teams that do not know what they are doing. You may get very anxious to umpire games with older and more skilled players that are more developed in their skills and can play higher quality baseball.

I mentioned earlier that when you are umpiring a good game, it often does not even seem like work. But in games where you just see ball after ball pitched and no action in the field you will sometimes find yourself counting down the minutes until the innings are over.

You must be patient because the time will come when you will be asked to umpire at games of older age groups and higher ability levels like tournaments. Those are the games where the real fun begins. Not only do tournaments pay more, but they provide more top-quality players and games and are a lot more fun to work. Those opportunities will just come as you learn the ropes and improve as an umpire. So be patient.

Umpire Partners - Most of the time, my partners are great, and I have fun working with them. But there are a few that are plain annoying. There is one dude I work with sometimes that has no clue what he is doing. He makes his calls very confidently, but they are usually wrong. I do not know what he's doing most of the time, and he confuses me when I work with him.

Once I was working with another partner and switched to this guy for the next game. My first partner took me aside and said: "Watch this guy, he's pretty new." But I knew the truth that he had been umpiring for more years than I had been an umpire! Just goes to show that some umpires get it, and others do not. You will just have to stay patient with those with lower aptitudes for seeing a play and hope you avoid getting assigned to work with them often!

Technique

Slightly different from mechanics, a technique is your personal style for calling plays such as strikes, balls, outs and safe calls. You want to develop a call for each that is the same every time, and that you feel comfortable doing. It's all about feeling and looking confident. When you develop a technique that seems right to you, you are not worried about looking weird or what people are thinking about you.

Your technique can differ depending on how close a call is, too. For example, I have diverse ways of calling an out at first base depending on if it is a close call or an easy out. For an easy out, I usually just point to the bag and then make the "out" signal. But if the call is close, I will firmly call "Out!" and gesture big and vigorously. I use more body language for close calls. And sometimes, I feed off the reactions of the crowd by making it a little fun with a crazy or energetic call.

Having an active call on close plays will help you look more decisive, which can reduce the chance of a dispute. There will still be one side that is not happy about the call and may dispute it, but being confident and firm does help.

Parents

Parents can be a real pain at times. The best advice I can give is to ignore them. You do not have to listen to them, and that's it. But if they get terrible and start swearing at you (yes, they do that sometimes) you have a couple of choices. First, I would suggest having a word with the team's coach and give them the initial opportunity to get the parents to settle down. They are usually willing and able to do that. The coach will say something like "Hey shut up over there!" The parents typically follow his request.

If the coach can't stop them, you have full authority to eject a parent immediately, without warning, especially if they are swearing. If you want to be nice and give a warning, handle it the same as with an arguing coach. But, know that you are not required to give a warning. Your job as an umpire is not just to officiate the game, but to help provide the kids with a pleasant experience. If you have parents swearing and yelling at you, you must lead by example and deal with it promptly and swiftly if the coach does not.

Mistakes

Mistakes happen in umpiring. At first, they will happen a lot. Later, mistakes will happen when you least expect them to. That's how you learn and get better—from your mistakes. Here are some of the most common mistakes made early on, all of which I have experienced myself:

Forgetting the Infield Fly Rule - Forgetting the infield fly rule is one of the most common mistakes for new umpires, but you won't make it very often. It usually results in chaos because kids are running all over the place and then everyone starts yelling.

The infield fly rule happens if there are runners on first and second, or bases are loaded, and there are less than two outs. If a pop fly goes into the infield, the umpire is supposed to call the batter automatically out. The purpose of the rule is so that the fielder cannot just let the pop fly drop and then get a double play on two runners who had to stay on the bases. So, you call the batter out as though the ball was caught. It also helps prevent mass chaos when smaller less able kids drop the ball in the infield, and everything just goes nuts. Better to just remember the infield fly rule and keep it all under control.

Hesitation - If a play is close, a new umpire may delay his call for a few seconds while going back and forth in his mind trying to decide what the call should be. Is he safe or is he out? By the time he decides, everyone is shouting, "Oh come on you don't know what you're talking about. That was totally wrong!" The same thing goes with calling strikes. If you hesitate from your usual timing on calling strikes—if you have any moment of hesitation—you may as well not call it. It will give the impression that you are not sure, and people will grab onto that.

A couple of things can help you improve in this area if you are the kind of person that tends to evaluate slowly before making a call:

- **Talk to yourself** That's right. Tell yourself you are confident of your judgment and calls. You will gain confidence and assertiveness over time knowing what you want to call without questioning yourself.

- **Be consistent** Your consistency is vital to the game, especially when you are assigned to work behind the home plate. If you keep the same strike zone, and the same time between a pitch and your call, people will sense that is your style, and they will believe you know what you're doing because your calls are consistent.

Being in the wrong position to make the call
— As I mentioned before, the mistake of being in the wrong position to make a call is mechanics and something that you need to learn over time. I've already mentioned some things to watch out for in the field, and you will find out more as time goes on.

There are specific stances to take behind the plate to see

the pitch too. You should put one foot right behind the catcher and your other foot a little bit in front so that you can set up to look around the catcher even if he's taller than you. I'm 5 foot 7, and the catcher is often taller than me. And so, yeah, I had to learn the right stance to see around him because there is just a little slot to see through.

You will also have to get an effective routine for when to squat down behind the plate. There is no particular time as a general rule to begin your squat, but when the pitcher throws the ball you'd better be there! I usually wait until the pitcher comes to his full set position.

There are a lot of mechanics you will need to learn, like where to stand if someone is stealing home and all the different posts in the field. It would be next to impossible to cover everything in this guide. And, since you will learn much more quickly from video demonstration, I would like to invite you to visit the **LIFETIME FREE BONUS AREA** containing links to videos covering the most critical positions you will need to master. Visit **http://producemybook.com/umpbonusreg** to get started.

Stick with it

At times, you may feel like you will never catch on to everything required to be a successful umpire, but you will. At some point, you will stop getting advice from senior mentors, and all of a sudden newer guys will start asking you for help.

Remember, you are never too old or too experienced to

learn. Recently, I had a 70-year-old who was just starting out in umpiring as my partner. He kept asking me if he was doing it right. It felt funny that a 19-year-old was helping a 70-year-old, but he didn't act like it was weird; he just seemed grateful for the advice.

I had someone mentoring me for the first year, and it helped me a lot. It needs to be a good umpire and someone who is not afraid to tell you what you need to work on and how to fix a problem you are obviously doing incorrectly. So, if you are not provided with an umpire mentor, seek people out as you work with them and ask for help.

My mentor was a scary dude. He was an ex-marine – a massive muscular bald dude. I had no problem doing whatever he said! But I learned so much. So, don't be afraid of an authoritarian type of umpire as your trainer or mentor. There are a lot of umpires that are very strict and even bossy sounding when they are training new umpires. Usually, they know their stuff. So, listen carefully and try to learn from them.

PART 7: HOW TO KEEP GETTING JOBS

Assignors have a lot on their plate every week because they have a ton of games to fill with umpires. If an umpire doesn't show up or does a lousy job, it can affect an entire tournament. Every game should have two umpires working to make the playing field fair for all the teams.

An assignor rarely meets all his umpires in person, so don't feel like you are being avoided or left out if you are not formally introduced. Although sometimes challenging to make a good impression on your assignor, look for opportunities to do so. You will get more games assigned to you, and therefore make more money, if you can build a positive reputation for your name in the assignor's mind. The following section has some tips on how you can meet and even exceed the assignor's expectations so that you are always top-of-mind when it's time for assigning new games.

Assignors Never Forget

I see my assignors rarely, if at all. Tournaments happen on fields all over the metropolitan area where I live, and an assignor can't possibly be at all of the games at the same time. But they have a good memory. One of my tournament assignors knows me and talks to me every time he sees me, but I barely know him. It's weird. He knows my name and where I went to high school and everything. But I've seen him, like, five times in three years. When I do recognize him, he comes over immediately and says hi and I'm hoping he's not going to yell at me for something I did wrong. But he'll just say, "Hi Rich, how's it going?" or something like that. I hardly talk to him, and he still somehow knows who I am.

My point is not that I'm so unforgettable, but just the opposite. Assignors want to work with people they can count on. The more you build a good reputation with your assignor, the better off you will be.

Whether your assignor likes you or not will not affect whether you get to umpire games. There are plenty of games the assignor needs to fill each week. But I do think that the more reliable you are at showing up and doing your job, the better the games you are assigned. For example, you may be assigned to the 11-12-year-old bracket instead of 8-10. So, the quality of your games is better and more interesting. If you say you are available all weekend, the assignor will give you a lot of games, which, of course, translates to more money!

Assignors Love Umpires That Do the Following:

1. Show reliability
2. Answer phone calls, texts, and emails promptly
3. Show up on time
4. Don't complain
5. Are friendly and approachable to their umpire partners
6. Don't provoke complaints from coaches

Absolutely Avoid the Following:

1. Not showing up to a game you accepted.

No excuse is permitted including getting a flat tire, becoming suddenly sick, or that you had to drive your mom to the airport for a funeral. At the very least, you will be fined and warned for a no-show. If you do it more than once, you probably simply will not get assigned to any more games. If something comes up that you really cannot avoid, even a true emergency, let the assignor know as soon as possible (before the game) and even try to find a replacement on your own.

2. Losing your temper at games. No cussing at kids, coaches or parents is tolerated, and DO NOT EVER HIT SOMEONE unless it is in self-defense. You will never work as an umpire again if you do any of these things.

CONCLUSION

Umpiring is not the perfect part-time job for everyone. It takes a lot of work to do the job well, and there are things about it (like with any job) that can be a real pain, like the weather or a boring game. For those who love baseball as I do, though, it is the best part-time job a teenager could ask for!

There are a lot of guys out there who have been umpiring a long time and are just excellent at it. I remember one umpire that I worked with a few times a couple of years ago. He was another one of those big bald guys that looked like he could scare the pants off you. But he was a veteran umpire who taught me a lot about mechanics. He was very friendly with parents after the game and told me that when parents or fans say "Thanks, Blue, good job," he always answers, "Thank you for coming out to support the kids." He said that always reminds him, as well as parents, that the point of the game is to give the kids a wonderful experience.

There are a lot of benefits to choosing to umpire as your part-time job. I've mentioned several times that the pay is high compared to other part-time jobs. I get paid to be around a sport that I've loved my whole life. And umpiring gives you a lot of power. You oversee everybody out there on the field including the coaches. As a teenager, that's fun to experience and necessary to learn how to manage. Umpiring is also an excellent way to stay physically healthy and mentally challenged.

I can still remember one game that I umpired that just felt like the perfect game. I was umpiring the 11-year-old bracket, and the teams were number one and two in the state. We went the full six innings in about an hour and 15 minutes, and the score was only 2 to 1. It was a crazy game with a lot of field plays. The best part was when we all walked off the field, everyone was happy, including the team that lost. No stupid thing made them lose; it was just the fact that the other side happened to beat them that day.

That's what makes the job worth it all - when you have a good game that goes all innings and is difficult to call, but in the end, everyone from both sides still says, "Good job." Umpiring truly is the greatest part-time job in the world for teenagers.

While this is the end of the book, I hope you will stay in touch! If you enjoyed *Teenage Baseball Umpire: How to Make Great Part-Time Money and Have Fun at Your Job Too*, please take the time to provide a review on your Amazon account for this book.

Every parent and teenager baseball enthusiast should know the great opportunities available to them through baseball umpiring. Your review will be helpful toward sharing that important message throughout the U.S. Very few people take the time to supply written reviews, so it is a huge deal if you do. I very much appreciate it.

Please connect with Rich Dossan through our main email address at **crew@producemybook.com** and be sure to register for free for your free LIFETIME access to the bonus area. To get started, register now at **http://producemybook.com/umpbonusreg**.

Other Books You May Be Interested In:

Rookie Season: How to Coach a Youth Baseball Team for the First Time...and Win More than Just Games by Randy Treeman, available at ProduceMyBook.com

Be sure to visit ProduceMyBook.com to find our other quality indie non-fiction books.

☐

RICH DOSSAN

LIFETIME FREE NEXT-STEPS BONUS!

Our aim at ProduceMyBook.com is to provide every step, tool, and resource possible for you to take the next step toward becoming a successful teenage youth baseball umpire. The author, Rich Dossan, has supplied us with a full suite of getting-started coaching documents, recommended videos, game situation quizzes and equipment reviews for your use. We have carefully compiled these valuable resources into a bonus area for you to access online whenever you wish. Some of the bonus items are described in the book, but others are not. So, be sure to get your LIFETIME free access to the bonus area. Visit **http://producemybook.com/umpbonusreg** to register for free.

Made in the USA
Monee, IL
20 October 2020